LIVING WITH DISEASES AND DISORDERS

Muscular Dystrophy and Other Neuromuscular Disorders

LIVING WITH DISEASES AND DISORDERS

ADHD and Other Behavior Disorders

Allergies and Other Immune System Disorders

Asthma, Cystic Fibrosis, and Other Respiratory Disorders

Autism and Other Developmental Disorders

Cancer and Sickle Cell Disease

Cerebral Palsy and Other Traumatic Brain Injuries

Crohn's Disease and Other Digestive Disorders

Depression, Anxiety, and Bipolar Disorders

Diabetes and Other Endocrine Disorders

Migraines and Seizures

Muscular Dystrophy and Other Neuromuscular Disorders

LIVING WITH DISEASES AND DISORDERS

Muscular Dystrophy and Other Neuromuscular Disorders

MOLLY JONES

SERIES ADVISOR
HEATHER L. PELLETIER, Ph.D.

Pediatric Psychologist, Hasbro Children's Hospital
Clinical Assistant Professor, Warren Alpert Medical School of Brown University

MASON CREST

Mason Crest
450 Parkway Drive, Suite D
Broomall, PA 19008
www.masoncrest.com

MTM Publishing, Inc.
435 West 23rd Street, #8C
New York, NY 10011
www.mtmpublishing.com

President: Valerie Tomaselli
Vice President, Book Development: Hilary Poole
Designer: Annemarie Redmond
Copyeditor: Peter Jaskowiak
Editorial Assistant: Leigh Eron

Series ISBN: 978-1-4222-3747-2
Hardback ISBN: 978-1-4222-3758-8
E-Book ISBN: 978-1-4222-8039-3

Library of Congress Cataloging-in-Publication Data
Names: Jones, Molly, 1933– author.
Title: Muscular dystrophy and other neuromuscular disorders / by Molly Jones; series consultant, Heather Pelletier, PhD Hasbro Children's Hospital, Alpert Medical School/ Brown University.
Description: Broomall, PA: Mason Crest, [2018] | Series: Living with diseases and disorders | Audience: Age 12+ | Audience: Grade 7 to 8. | Includes index.
Identifiers: LCCN 2017000437 (print) | LCCN 2017002184 (ebook) | ISBN 9781422237588 (hardback: alk. paper) | ISBN 9781422280393 (ebook)
Subjects: LCSH: Muscular dystrophy—Juvenile literature. | Neuromuscular diseases— Juvenile literature.
Classification: LCC RC935.M7 J66 2018 (print) | LCC RC935.M7 (ebook) | DDC 616.7/48—dc23
LC record available at https://lccn.loc.gov/2017000437

Printed and bound in the United States of America.

First printing
9 8 7 6 5 4 3 2 1

TABLE OF CONTENTS

Key Icons to Look for:

Words to Understand: These words with their easy-to-understand definitions will increase the reader's understanding of the text, while building vocabulary skills.

Sidebars: This boxed material within the main text allows readers to build knowledge, gain insights, explore possibilities, and broaden their perspectives by weaving together additional information to provide realistic and holistic perspectives.

Educational Videos: Readers can view videos by scanning our QR codes, which will provide them with additional educational content to supplement the text. Examples include news coverage, moments in history, speeches, iconic sports moments, and much more.

Text-Dependent Questions: These questions send the reader back to the text for more careful attention to the evidence presented there.

Research Projects: Readers are pointed toward areas of further inquiry connected to each chapter. Suggestions are provided for projects that encourage deeper research and analysis.

Series Glossary of Key Terms: This back-of-the-book glossary contains terminology used throughout the series. Words found here increase the reader's ability to read and comprehend higher-level books and articles in this field.

SERIES INTRODUCTION

According to the Chronic Disease Center at the Centers for Disease Control and Prevention, over 100 million Americans suffer from a chronic illness or medical condition. In other words, they have a health problem that lasts three months or more, affects their ability to perform normal activities, and requires frequent medical care and/or hospitalizations. Epidemiological studies suggest that between 15 and 18 million of those with chronic illness or medical conditions are children and adolescents. That's roughly one out of every four children in the United States.

These young people must exert more time and energy to complete the tasks their peers do with minimal thought. For example, kids with Crohn's disease, ulcerative colitis, or other digestive issues have to plan meals and snacks carefully, to make sure they are not eating food that could irritate their stomachs or cause pain and discomfort. People with cerebral palsy, muscular dystrophy, or other physical limitations associated with a medical condition may need help getting dressed, using the bathroom, or joining an activity in gym class. Those with cystic fibrosis, asthma, or epilepsy may have to avoid certain activities or environments altogether. ADHD and other behavior disorders require the individual to work harder to sustain the level of attention and focus necessary to keep up in school.

Living with a chronic illness or medical condition is not easy. Identifying a diagnosis and adjusting to the initial shock is only the beginning of a long journey. Medications, follow-up appointments and procedures, missed school or work, adjusting to treatment regimens, coping with uncertainty, and readjusting expectations are all hurdles one has to overcome in learning how to live one's best life. Naturally, feelings of sadness or anxiety may set in while learning how to make it all work. This is especially true for young people, who may reach a point in their medical journey when they have to rethink some of their original goals and life plans to better match their health reality.

Chances are, you know people who live this reality on a regular basis. It is important to remember that those affected by chronic illness are family members, neighbors, friends, or maybe even our own doctors. They are likely navigating the demands of the day a little differently, as they balance the specific accommodations necessary to manage their illness. But they have the same desire to be productive and included as those who are fortunate not to have a chronic illness.

This set provides valuable information about the most common childhood chronic illnesses, in language that is engaging and easy for students to grasp. Each chapter highlights important vocabulary words and offers text-dependent questions to help assess comprehension. Meanwhile, educational videos (available by scanning QR codes) and research projects help connect the text to the outside world.

Our mission with this set is twofold. First, the volumes provide a go-to source for information about chronic illness for young people who are living with particular conditions. Each volume in this set strives to provide reliable medical information and practical advice for living day-to-day with various challenges. Second, we hope these volumes will also help kids without chronic illness better understand and appreciate how people with health challenges live. After all, if one in four young people is managing a health condition, it's safe to assume that the majority of our youth already know someone with a chronic illness, whether they realize it or not.

With the growing presence of social media, bullying is easier than ever before. It's vital that young people take a moment to stop and think about how they are more similar to kids with health challenges than they are different. Poor understanding and low tolerance for individual differences are often the platforms for bullying and noninclusive behavior, both in person and online. Living with Diseases and Disorders strives to close the gap of misunderstanding.

The ultimate solution to the bullying problem is surely an increase in empathy. We hope these books will help readers better understand and appreciate not only the daily struggles of people living with chronic conditions, but their triumphs as well.

—Heather Pelletier, Ph.D.
Hasbro Children's Hospital
Warren Alpert Medical School of Brown University

WORDS TO UNDERSTAND

biopsy: the removal and laboratory study of a small piece of living tissue.

carrier: a person who does not experience a disease but can pass it on to offspring.

chromosome: a threadlike structure found in the nucleus of most living cells, carrying genetic information in the form of genes.

Duchenne muscular dystrophy: a type of muscular dystrophy that occurs usually in males.

dystrophin: a protein essential for growing healthy muscles

involuntary muscle: a muscle that functions without conscious direction.

muscle wasting: the loss of muscle tissue.

mutation: a change to the structure of a gene.

neuromuscular: related to the nerve–muscle connection.

neurophysiology: related to the functions of the nervous system and its connections with the physical body.

voluntary muscle: a muscle that a person can move at will.

CHAPTER ONE

What Is a Neuromuscular Disorder?

Dan is a busy young man. He operates an upbeat website and blog, sharing his life with others and encouraging others to live their own lives fully. He drives a wheelchair-accessible truck, lives and travels independently, and plays professional wheelchair tennis.

Dan was diagnosed at age 13 with a form of muscular dystrophy (MD). Since then, he has found ways of doing as many of the things he has wanted to do in life as possible, in spite of his challenging diagnosis. You can find out more about Dan and his busy life at musculardystrophybook.com.

Before Dan's diagnosis, his life was very different. He didn't think much about whether he'd be able to move his fingers to button his shirt. He wasn't worried about keeping his shoulders, head, or feet from moving when he wanted them to be still. And playing tennis and basketball were not problems for him, either. One day, however, his life began to change, as his muscles began to grow weaker and harder to control.

Roughly 1 in 35,000 boys has some form of MD.

People like Dan have neuromuscular disorders (NMDs), and daily tasks and activities may at times be a struggle for them. If you or someone you know is in that situation, learning as much as possible about the particular type of disorder will help you find the best ways to approach life's challenges. It will help you to understand what's going on in the affected parts of the body, what has caused this change, and what the future holds.

Neuromuscular disorders include a wide range of conditions in which nerves fail to give correct signals to one or more of the body's muscle groups. Dozens of different neuromuscular disorders have been recognized and described by medical researchers. Each one causes its own pattern of movement problems because of the nerves and muscles involved. Of these disorders, muscular dystrophy (MD) occurs most often. Muscular dystrophy itself is an umbrella term for more than thirty distinct genetic diseases. Of these, the most common type is Duchenne muscular dystrophy (DMD).

All neuromuscular disorders, even DMD, are rare conditions. Approximately 1 out of every 35,000 boys born worldwide will have some type of MD. The conditions occur even less frequently for girls, who very rarely acquire DMD. However, girls are subject to other types of NMDs.

Each type of neuromuscular disease, including MD, is a genetic disease caused by a gene mutation. NMDs are not contagious, so a person with MD cannot transmit the disorder to another person—except from a parent to a child through the parent's genes.

Genetics and MD

The muscle problems that come with muscular dystrophy are caused by an accidental, random event called a mutation, which changes the functioning of a gene that controls that particular muscle or muscle group. The mutation disrupts the way the gene normally sends signals to the muscle. This damage can occur

GENES AND HOW YOU BECAME YOU

Human beings inherit traits, such as height, hair color, eye color, and the shape of facial features, from their parents. These traits are determined at the time of conception, when a sperm cell is united with an egg cell, creating a new human being. Information about these traits is carried in genes. Some traits are determined by a single pair of genes, one from each parent; other, more complex, traits involve many genes.

Every cell in the body contains a nucleus, and within each nucleus are 46 microscopic, threadlike chromosomes, 23 from each parent. These 23 pairs of chromosomes carry the genes inherited from each parent. Each pair of chromosomes carries tens of thousands of paired genes. Traits resulting from all but one of these 23 pairs of chromosomes are unrelated to whether they came from the male or female parent.

In that one pair of chromosomes, called the X and Y chromosomes, the source may matter. For example, the gene that determines whether a child will be male or female is found on the male chromosome of that 23rd pair. The male parent has one X-chromosome and one Y-chromosome. The female parent has two X-chromosomes. Therefore a female will always pass on a gene from an X chromosome, but the male will pass on genes from his X chromosome about half the time, and from his Y chromosome about half the time. If the male passes on a gene from the Y-chromosome, the child will then have one X and one Y gene, and will therefore be male. If the male passes on a gene from the X-chromosome, the child will have two X genes, one from each parent, and will therefore be female.

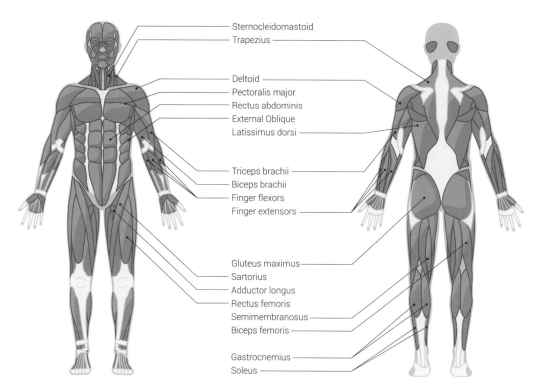

The muscular system.

in more than one way. For example, the person may have inherited an already damaged gene from a parent. Or the damage could have occurred from a gene mutation at the time of conception. Either way, the damage leaves the gene and the muscles it was intended to control unable to function as originally intended.

Muscles are primarily made of proteins. The protein produced by the **dystrophin** gene is essential for growing healthy muscle tissue. When a gene associated with producing healthy dystrophin is damaged, the damage causes some muscle protein to be missing or incorrectly formed. This affects the health and strength of the muscle. Since the dystrophin gene sends signals to the muscle, a mutation on the dystrophin gene can result in a type of MD. This loss and weakening of muscle tissue will continue to get worse over time, and, unfortunately, the resulting disability will also grow worse.

Duchenne muscular dystrophy (DMD) is caused by a mutation on a gene from the X chromosome inherited from the female parent. With two X chromosomes, a healthy female child will have a pair of healthy X-related **dystrophin** genes. If a female child has one damaged dystrophin gene, her healthy second dystrophin gene is usually able to overcome effects from the damaged gene. She will become a **carrier** of MD, but won't experience the disease fully. But a male child with one damaged dystrophin gene doesn't have the advantage of a second X-related dystrophin gene. He will experience the full effects of MD.

Types of MD

The effects on people who have various types of MD vary widely, depending on which gene is damaged and which muscles they involve. Below are descriptions of several of the many types of MD.

- *Duchenne muscular dystrophy* (DMD) symptoms include general muscle weakness and **muscle wasting**, or a loss of muscle mass and strength. DMD eventually involves all voluntary muscles, most especially the pelvis and the arms and legs. Usually cases of DMD are recognized by the time kids are about five years old, but sometimes DMD isn't diagnosed until kids reach school age. By that time, their posture and way of walking will begin to show the typical MD characteristics. These include a tendency to walk on the toes or forward part of the feet, a waddling gait (a side-to-side rocking motion that helps maintain balance), enlarged calf muscles, clumsiness and frequent falls, and difficulty raising the arms.

    Children with DMD frequently require a wheelchair by the time they are between ages 7 and 12. Eventually, DMD can cause weakened heart muscles and respiratory (breathing) complications, both of which contribute to a shortened life span. It is unusual for a person with DMD to survive beyond their 30s, but in some cases they do.

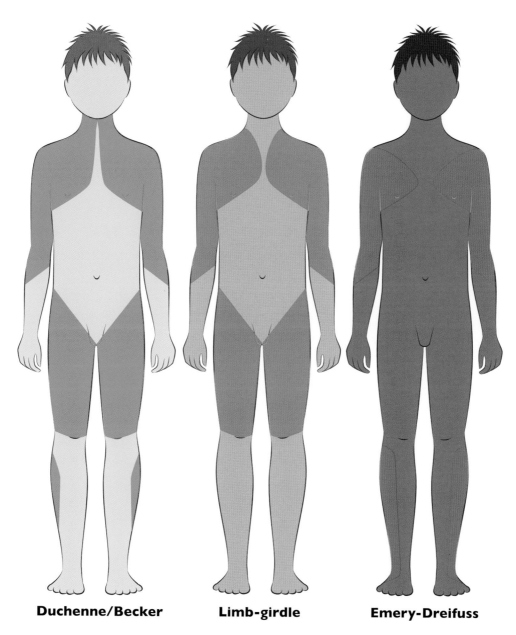

Duchenne/Becker **Limb-girdle** **Emery-Dreifuss**

Three types of MD; commonly affected muscles are in red.

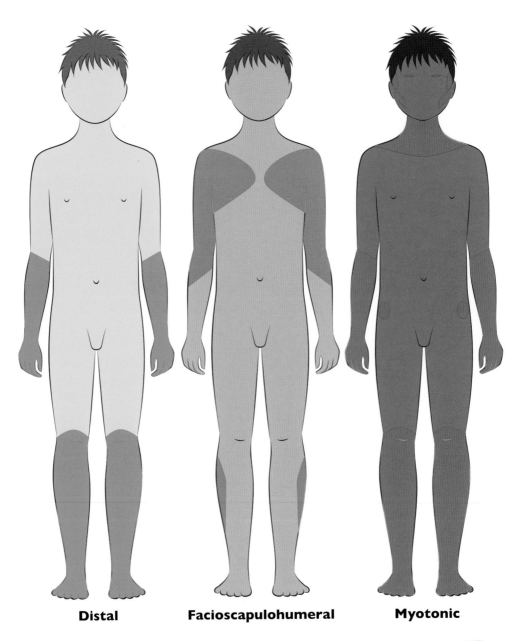

| Distal | Facioscapulohumeral | Myotonic |

Three other types of MD, with commonly affected muscles marked. In myotonic MD, there is some variation as to what muscles are affected, depending on whether the person has type 1 or type 2.

- *Becker muscular dystrophy* follows a path similar to Duchenne, but it results in symptoms that are less serious than in Duchenne. A German doctor, Peter Emil Becker, first described this variant of DMD in the 1950s.

- *Limb-girdle muscular dystrophy* (LGMD) is a type of MD that can appear at any time from late childhood to middle age. Symptoms of LGMD include muscle weakness and wasting. The muscles affected at first are those around the shoulders and pelvic area. The disease then progresses slowly to other areas of the body. The name "limb-girdle" refers to the tough tissue that attaches a limb, such as an arm or leg, to the trunk or main part of the body. If a person with LGMD develops breathing difficulties or heart complications, their life span may be shortened.

- *Myotonic muscular dystrophy* (MMD) appears in early adulthood. There are two types of myotonic MD. Type 1 particularly affects the lower legs, hands, neck, and face. Type 2 primarily involves muscles of the neck, shoulders, elbows, and hips. In myotonic MD, a patient typically finds it hard to relax muscles that have been tightened or contracted.

- *Emery-Dreifuss muscular dystrophy* (EDMD) may appear in childhood to the early teens. As you can see in the diagram on page 15, EDMD causes problems with shoulder muscles, as well as the upper arms and the shins. Joint deformities are common, progress is slow, and sudden death may occur from cardiac problems. EDMD is named for the researchers

EDUCATIONAL VIDEO

Scan this code for a video about walking with limb-girdle muscular dystrophy.

Alan Eglin H. Emery and Fritz E. Dreifuss, who recognized and described it as a separate disease.

- *Distal muscular dystrophy* (DD) usually appears between ages 40 and 60. Distal MD can be caused by a mutation in any one of eight different genes. The name *distal* describes the usual places where disease symptoms begin—away from the points where limbs attach to the body. Symptoms begin in the hands or feet, in other words, and include weakness and wasting of the muscles of the hands, forearms, and lower legs. The disease progresses slowly, and though the affected person experiences discomfort, they rarely become completely disabled.

- *Facioscapulohumeral muscular dystrophy* (FSHD) can come about at almost any age, but it usually becomes apparent during the teenage years. The long name comes from the parts of the body most severely affected. Muscle weakness usually begins in the face and shoulders. People with FSH may not close their eyelids completely when sleeping and may not be able to whistle. Also, their shoulder blades may appear somewhat malformed.

Voluntary and Involuntary Muscles

With your thigh muscles, you raise your knees and swing your legs forward when you walk or run; with your neck muscles, you turn your head from side to side. With your shoulder muscles you raise your arms, while your jaw muscles enable you to chew. These are examples of voluntary muscles, muscles you can control at will to move various limbs and body parts. There are 434 voluntary muscles in the human body.

Involuntary muscles are those that function outside of a person's conscious control. The brain directly controls their actions and movements without the person's conscious control. The heart muscle and the smooth muscle around the intestinal wall are examples of involuntary muscles. Lung muscles are

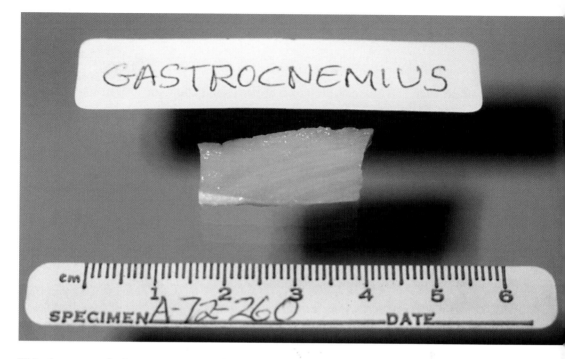

This tissue sample from someone with DMD shows yellowish fat that has replaced muscle tissue.

considered involuntary; even if you consciously choose not to breathe, your lungs will keep you breathing when you are not paying attention.

The muscles affected by NMDs, including MD, are mostly voluntary muscles. However, in some cases, the condition eventually affects involuntary muscles. DMD, LGMD, EDMD, and Becker MD are examples of disorders that can affect the involuntary muscles of the heart.

Diagnosing Muscular Dystrophy

No one wants to be told they or their child has muscular dystrophy. At the same time, knowing as much as possible about the patient's specific disorder will help get the best available treatment and have the best possible future. A careful examination by a physician followed by laboratory tests can make an accurate diagnosis possible.

First, a patient with MD will have weaker muscles than a healthy boy his age usually has. The muscles may also appear somewhat **wasted**. In some cases, though, muscles become enlarged instead of wasted, especially the calf muscles. But even if they are larger than is typical, the calves are still weaker. Their larger size is due to fat replacing the lost muscle tissue.

In a very young boy, the doctor will be interested in his posture and how he moves. He will ask the parents if the patient was late in standing or starting to walk. Other reasons for concern would include whether the patient has trouble getting up from the floor without help, whether his shoulder muscles are weak, and whether he continues to have trouble walking. Some children with MD develop a waddling gait when they are still very young.

If the patient is a male, and the doctor has noticed one or more of these typical MD traits, both doctor and parents may suspect he has MD. To be sure, after the exam and a review of the child's history, the doctor will use lab studies and possibly a **neurophysiology** exam to support a diagnosis of MD. In the neurophysiology exam, a doctor will examine traits such as the boy's gait, coordination, and alertness. One reason for this exam is to rule out other possible causes of the patient's symptoms that would need very different treatments from those for MD. Lab tests useful for diagnosis include muscle and nerve **biopsies**, genetic testing, and a blood test to detect a deficiency of creatine in the child's muscle tissue. Creatine is an enzyme that leaks out of damaged muscles. When creatine levels in the blood are high, it usually means muscle tissue is being lost and creatine is leaking out into the system.

Other Well-Known Neuromuscular Diseases

Many other neuromuscular diseases affect the lives of thousands of people and their families. Two that have recently affected prominent and well-known people are Parkinson's disease and amyotrophic lateral sclerosis (ALS, or Lou Gehrig's disease). Like DMD, these disorders are under intense study to discover cures and develop treatments to relieve symptoms that make life difficult.

ALS is a motor-neuron disease. It brings about the death of neurons, or nerve cells, that control voluntary muscles. People with ALS have stiffening muscles, twitching muscles, and increasing weakness as their muscles grow smaller. Up to 10 percent of cases are genetic, inherited from parents. In some cases, the disease has been connected with specific gene mutations, but in most cases the cause is not known. ALS usually sets in at about age 60, and most patients live 2 to 4 years after their diagnosis, though some live more than 10 more years. At this time, there is no cure for ALS.

ALS became known as Lou Gehrig's disease because of the famous baseball player who had it; here, Gehrig poses on the far left with fellow players at the 1937 All-Star Game.

Muhammad Ali receiving an award in 2012.

In Parkinson's disease, a loss of an important brain chemical called dopamine causes the nerves to lose their usual control of muscle movements. This loss results in muscle stiffening or muscle tremors in the face, arms, or legs.

A medication called L-dopa replaces some of the dopamine and lessens the severity of the symptoms for a period of time, but it does not cure the disease.

The public has become much more familiar with these disorders due to well-known people who've had ALS or Parkinson's disease. In fact, ALS is often referred to by its nickname, "Lou Gehrig's disease," after a popular baseball player in the 1930s who had the disease. The prominent physicist Stephen Hawking was diagnosed with ALS in 1963, and as of 2016, he was still alive and actively contributing to his field, despite being severely disabled physically.

In 1964, Muhammad Ali, at age 22, became the heavyweight boxing champion of the world. Ali was widely considered to be one of the most outstanding sports figures of the 20th century. Ali was diagnosed with Parkinson's disease in 1984. Some believed the many blows to the head he received in boxing caused brain damage that contributed to the condition. The actor Michael J. Fox is another celebrity who has Parkinson's, and his progress has been watched with concern by his fans. On multiple occasions, Ali and Fox appeared together to raise money for Parkinson's research, and to make the public more aware of the condition.

Text-Dependent Questions

1. Can you "catch" MD from a classmate?
2. How does an involuntary muscle differ from a voluntary muscle?
3. Is it possible to have MD if neither of your parents has it?

Research Project

Be a genetic detective: compare three of your physical traits, such as eye color, hair curliness, nose shape, or height, with the same traits in your parents and as many grandparents, aunts, uncles, and cousins as possible. Describe traits that appear to be genetically transmitted from one generation to the next.

WORDS TO UNDERSTAND

contraction: the squeezing and tightening of a muscle.

ventilator: a piece of electrical equipment that helps an MD patient take a larger amount of oxygen into their lungs.

CHAPTER TWO

Neuromuscular Disorders and Daily Life

Just as life with Duchenne muscular dystrophy (DMD) is not the same for every patient, neither is life with any other neuromuscular disorder. A young woman named Mandy Van Benthuysen, who was diagnosed at age four with limb-girdle muscular dystrophy (LGMD), described her life in an article published by the Muscular Dystrophy Association. Though the diagnosis left her parents in shock, they set about learning all they could about LGMD and making adjustments to their lives, individually and as a family. Before long, their life included doctors, braces, therapy, and learning new ways to do things.

In spite of having to work around barriers that continually popped up, Mandy was one of the lucky MD patients who was surrounded by family and had school and community support. Mandy remembers her childhood as being "wonderful." She graduated from college and now works in the television industry.

Mandy's experience is encouraging to others affected by a neuromuscular disorder. But there are many who are not as fortunate as Mandy is, who do not

Siblings can play vital roles in the support systems of people with MD.

have the support and resources she has had. If you are a person with MD, or you are a friend or family helper of someone with the disease, the Muscular Dystrophy Association (www.MDA.org) or the Americans with Disabilities Act website (www.ada.gov/) can help you find resources that are available to you and those who need assistance.

Most people with NMDs keep in regular contact with their doctors. Also, they may have a visiting nurse or therapist who helps with medications, physical therapy, exercise, and other aspects of daily life. A social worker may be assigned to the person with MD and the person's family to assist with needs such as arranging for household help or finding employment.

It's important to be fitted comfortably with braces, a walker or wheelchair, or other equipment if needed. Activities such as dressing in the morning for school are more complicated for a person with MD who uses assistive equipment. Bathing and eating always require more time for someone with MD. As one young adult male commented, "Because of my MD, it takes me 20 minutes every morning just to button my shirt, but I'm so proud when I've done it myself!"

The Importance of Therapy

Depending on the type of neuromuscular disorder a patient has and the stage of development of the disease, both exercise and physical therapy may be part of the person's day.

IMPORTANCE OF EXERCISE

According to Medscape and the consultants of the American College of Sports Medicine, a safe and effective exercise program can have a positive effect on symptoms of muscular dystrophy. Exercise for MD patients increases muscle strength and endurance, enhances mobility, stretches muscles to lessen muscle contraction, decreases the risk of falling, and improves balance and coordination. Before beginning regular exercise, patients and caregivers should discuss their plan with their doctors. Begin the plan slowly, and increase effort very gradually.

Kids with neuromuscular disorders can still participate in traditional schools.

DMD patients who depend on wheelchairs may experience respiratory failure in their late teens or early 20s. While not all cases of DMD affect heart function, many young men with DMD do start to have heart troubles by the time they are 18. This is why it's so important that DMD treatments take care to help strengthen both the lung muscles and the heart muscles.

Some of the therapy now offered to MD patients focuses on respiratory function. Researchers have developed a type of **ventilator** that helps increase the amount of oxygen the patient's weak lung muscles are able to draw into the lungs. One type of ventilator can be used while the patient is asleep.

The Importance of Education

Each person with MD has a unique combination of age, diagnosis, disease progress, family resources, and community opportunities. Working out the best educational plan for all patients is important for their future, and also to enrich their lives as much as possible as they live in the present. But for any particular MD child of school age, finding the best possible program and enabling the child to take part in it should be a high priority.

Some parents choose to home school their child with MD because of the complications of transportation and making suitable accommodations at school to meet the student's needs. On the other hand, some parents may believe their own level of education is not adequate for home schooling. Many parents need to work full time and cannot be at home for schooling. In some cases, the local school system can provide a teacher for a home-bound student.

There are many benefits to attending a public or private school, however, if the student's needs can be met there. Not only will the school program cost less, but it will also give the student an opportunity to make new friends. Kids with MD can learn to get along in new places and circumstances, and to function independently when no one is around to help.

Even when a student with MD can find ways of coping with the physical challenges of a school situation, not all the barriers are physical. The attitudes of other students may not be welcoming or helpful. Disabled students sometimes find themselves excluded from much of the fun others are having. Parents may have to choose between withdrawing their student and finding another school, or working with the school staff to create a more inclusive attitude and approach to making sure all students feel welcome and included.

DISCOVERING MD

Guillaume-Benjamin-Amand
Duchenne de Boulogne.

Many people have contributed to the knowledge and insights that have made life better for MD patients. But two researchers in particular illuminated the nature of MD disorders, opening the door to making progress in dealing with them.

Guillaume-Benjamin-Amand Duchenne de Boulogne (1806–1875), a French neurologist, has been credited as the first to recognize the nature of muscular dystrophy. However, a physician in England, Edward Meryon (1809–1880), had actually described muscular dystrophy in detail prior to the writings of Duchenne. Meryon accepted the name Duchenne muscular dystrophy, and he never tried to get equal credit for his work.

Text-Dependent Questions

1. Briefly describe two different types of challenges an NMD patient is likely to experience in a typical day.
2. Who first described the muscular dystrophy disorders?
3. Why is exercise important for people with MD?

EDUCATIONAL VIDEO

Scan this code for a video about researchers working on Duchenne MD.

Research Project

Plan a simple fitness program for a DMD patient. Websites of fitness experts can provide information such as www.musculardystrophyuk.org/assets/0001/1477/Physio_booklet_web.pdf where a sports medicine expert discusses exercise for those who have DMD. Do further research to include the views of more than one expert.

WORDS TO UNDERSTAND

amniotic fluid: the liquid that surrounds a fetus in the mother's womb.

clinical trial: a study in which the test subjects are human beings.

DNA: deoxyribonucleic acid, or DNA, is a molecule that carries the genetic instructions used in the growth and development of the individual.

genetic screening: studying an individual's genes to predict diseases or characteristics of offspring.

Human Genome Project: a cooperative science venture to identify and catalogue every human gene and its chromosomal location.

mdx mouse: a breed of mouse especially useful in testing drugs and procedures for humans.

stem cells: early-stage versatile cells that can give rise to multiple types of mature cells.

CHAPTER THREE

Looking to the Future

For patients with neuromuscular disorders and their families, the 21st century is a time for optimism. Only in recent decades have researchers and doctors offered real hope that they would soon understand the cause of these diseases.

New Understanding

Until a few years ago, many believed that a single cause would eventually explain all the types of muscular dystrophy. In fact, in the 19th century MD was defined as a single disease. When, in the 20th century, MD was broken out into smaller subcategories, many people still thought that there was one single cause, such as a lack of adequate blood supply to the affected muscle.

As researchers continued to study the muscle fibers in MD patients, the role of the protein dystrophin caught the researchers' attention. The word *dystrophy* originally came from two Greek words: *dys*, meaning abnormal or faulty, and *trophe*, meaning food or nourishment. Researchers found that dystrophin was clearly playing a part in patients' inability to move particular muscle groups.

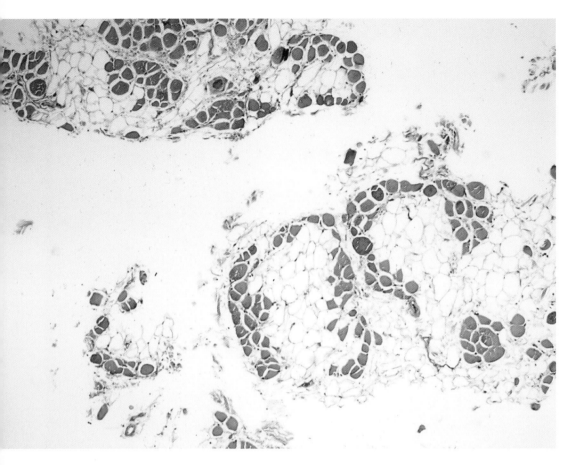

This image of muscle tissue from a person with DMD shows the muscle fibers (dark pink) being replaced by adipose cells (light pink).

In 1987, scientists discovered that dystrophin was absent in muscles affected by Duchenne muscular dystrophy (DMD). Since a lack of dystrophin results in muscle weakness and deterioration, this discovery led to more research and to our current, improved understanding of DMD. **Genetic screening** and therapy might someday prevent cases of DMD that result from an inherited gene mutation. But many cases (1 in 10,000) come about from a new mutation that occurs at conception. This means that genetic screening will never eliminate all cases of DMD. Consequently, it's really important to find new, more effective treatments.

Treating MD and Other NMDs

Since 1986, two major advances in biological research have brought new hope for eventually developing effective treatments for MD. First, the **Human Genome Project** discovered and catalogued the location and characteristics of each gene within the human **DNA**, or genetic material. This knowledge has enabled researchers to locate and study the genes responsible for each type of neuromuscular disorder. Second, the increased understanding of **stem cells** promised a growing range of medical applications.

Once researchers became aware of the central role of the protein dystrophin in muscular dystrophy, their new understanding also suggested a possible solution: replacing the defective gene. Several possible ways of inserting a new gene in place of the defective one have shown promise in the lab. Other approaches include testing ways to repair the genetic defects. In some cases, the mutation has caused a damaging process that prevents the cells from correctly following their genetic instructions. In these cases, the solution is to block the unwanted process. In still another approach, researchers have intervened to enable cells to remove defective DNA within their own nuclei, and thus make a self-correction.

Animals have long been valuable resources for studying human disease. What researchers have learned by enlisting animals in laboratory studies has changed the outlook for humans with neuromuscular diseases. In many pre-clinical trials, new procedures or medications have first been tested on animals. This approach has been used

EDUCATIONAL VIDEO

Scan this code for a video about ongoing work to treat Duchenne.

to ensure a medication's safety and estimate its effectiveness before testing it on human subjects in a **clinical trial**. A specific mouse species called the **mdx mouse** and a dog species with a form of MD known as golden retriever muscular dystrophy (GRMD) have been used in DMD lab studies. Both animals naturally lack dystrophin, so they are useful for testing gene therapy treatments in the lab before testing them in humans.

Both gene therapy and stem cell therapy have shown promise in laboratory settings for correcting genetic errors that bring about neuromuscular disorders. Stem cells are early-stage, versatile cells found in muscle tissue as well as other places in the body. These cells are important in research because they can give rise to mature muscle cells to replace or supplement cells that are weak or missing.

Mice have been used in medical research since the 1600s.

ANOTHER VIEW

PETA stands for People for the Ethical Treatment of Animals. An animal rights organization, PETA is probably best known for their campaigns to stop celebrities from wearing fur. But in fact, PETA members work to end what they view as abuse of animals in all sorts of contexts, including the entertainment world and, most controversially, in scientific research. PETA's president, Ingrid Newkirk, is famous for stating that "When it comes to feelings like hunger, pain, and thirst, a rat is a pig is a dog is a boy." In other words, PETA believes animals should not be exploited for any reason, and that any benefits to humans do not outweigh the rights of the animals.

PETA opposes all animal testing, whether it is for harmful chemicals in a product or the environment, performing basic research to extend knowledge, using research to solve a specific problem or need, or testing for education and training purposes. The group has made a variety of arguments against these practices. For instance, they argue that animal testing is a waste of time, since curing an animal of a particular disease in a laboratory setting is not the same as curing a human. They also complain that animal research is insufficiently regulated and, too often, simply redundant.

In a 1989 interview with *Vogue* magazine, Newkirk stated that even if animal testing could result in a cure for a devastating disease such as AIDS, PETA would still oppose it, regardless of the potential benefits.

Since certain dogs and mice both experience Duchenne muscular dystrophy, both have been used in DMD studies. In one study, a team of scientists from Italy and France collected stem cells from healthy dogs that can become healthy muscle cells. They also collected cells from the dogs with MD, and then injected those dogs with the healthy stem cells. After a series of injections, four out of six MD dogs improved significantly in muscle strength and functioning. Other studies have also been encouraging in the effort to develop safe and effective treatments for human MD patients.

At this time, there is still no cure for Duchenne MD or any other neuromuscular disorder, nor is there an available treatment doctors can routinely prescribe. Yet dedicated doctors and scientists are constantly at work to make lives better for those with an NMD. The Muscular Dystrophy Association strongly supports research to gain understanding, develop effective treatments, and make progress toward curing neuromuscular disorders. The latest news about developments in neuromuscular research and better living for NMD patients can be found on the organization's website (www.MDA.org).

Transplants

A lively area of research in NMD treatments involves transplantation, or injecting muscle components from healthy donors into MD muscles.

In modern medicine, transplanting tissue or an entire body organ, such as a heart, lung, or kidney, from one person's body to another has become almost an everyday procedure. Yet one problem faces every organ recipient and their doctors: dealing with tissue rejection. Each person's body and its immune system are naturally programmed to reject foreign substances, or substances that did not originate in the recipient's body. Muscle transplants in MD patients face this same challenge.

Don't be afraid to ask your health-care provider about any questions or concerns you might have. They are there to help.

To address this problem, researchers have tried injecting repaired tissue from the MD patient's own muscle back into his or her body. Although this cuts down on rejection, the response using the patient's repaired tissue has not been as successful as using healthy tissue from a non-MD donor. Research continues on transplants in general—and on transplanting muscle tissue in MD patients in particular—in hopes of finding more effective ways of avoiding tissue rejection.

ORGANIZATIONS

There are a large number of organizations with the mission of helping people with MD.

Coalition to Cure Calpain 3 (C3)
15 Compo Parkway
Westport, CT 06880
email: info@curecalpain3.org
web: www.curecalpain3.org
tel: 203-221-1611

Cure CMD
P.O. Box 701
Olathe, KS 66051
email: info@curecmd.com
web: www.curecmd.org
tel: 424-265-0874

Facioscapulohumeral Muscular Dystrophy (FSH) Society
64 Grove Street
Watertown, MA 02472
email: info@fshsociety.org
web: www.fshsociety.org
tel: 617-658-7877

Jain Foundation
9725 Third Avenue NE
Suite 204
Seattle, WA 98115
email: admin@jain-foundation
web: www.jain-foundation.org
tel: 425-882-1440

Stem Cell and Gene Therapy

In research, both gene therapy and stem cell therapy have been used successfully to treat a variety of disorders. The dream of scientists who work in gene therapy is that one day we will be able to replace or repair the faulty genetic material that causes illness. Researchers believe that new

Muscular Dystrophy Association

National Office

222 S. Riverside Plaza

Suite 1500

Chicago, IL 60606

email: mda@mdausa.org

web: www.mda.org

tel: 800-572-1717

Muscular Dystrophy Family Foundation (MDFF)

1033 Third Avenue SW Ste 108

Carmel, IN 46032

web: www.mdff.org

tel: 317-695-9140

Myotonic Dystrophy Foundation

1004 O'Reilly Avenue

San Francisco, CA 94129

email: info@myotonic.org

web: www.myotonic.org

tel: 86-MYOTONIC; 415-800-7777

National Institute of Arthritis and Musculoskeletal and Skin Diseases (NIAMS)

National Institutes of Health, DHHS

31 Center Dr.

Rm. 4C02 MSC 2350

Bethesda, MD 20892-2350

email: NIAMSinfo@mail.nih.gov

web: www.niams.nih.gov

tel: 877-22-NIAMS (226-4267)

Parent Project Muscular Dystrophy (PPMD)

401 Hackensack Avenue

9th Floor

Hackensack, NJ 07601

email: info@parentprojectmd.org

web: www.parentprojectmd.org

tel: 800-714-KIDS (5437)

genetic material can be inserted into a sick person's DNA, to enable their bodies to fight off diseases. In theory, there is no end to the diseases gene therapy could potentially cure. But in practice, the science is too new and the techniques too risky for gene therapy to be used outside of a laboratory. There are also serious ethical questions to be worked out: for instance, who decides what is "necessary" gene therapy and what isn't? Nevertheless,

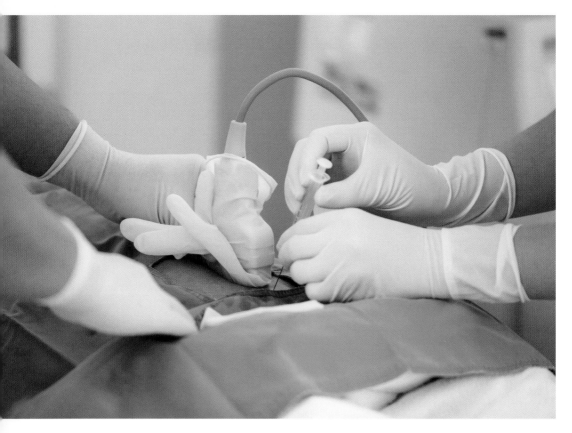

In a procedure called amniocentesis, a bit of the fluid surrounding a fetus is removed with a needle and then analyzed. Researchers hope amniotic fluid can also be a great help in developing MD treatments.

clinical trials are underway to test the effectiveness of gene therapy in a number of different diseases, including Duchenne MD.

Amniotic fluid is a rich source of multi-use stem cells that can grow to become new bone, cartilage, muscle, or spinal disc material, as well as other types of tissue. Unlike embryonic stem cells, stem cells from amniotic fluid can be collected from a pregnant woman without harming her developing baby, even while doing routine testing during pregnancy or at the time of birth.

In studies, injections of human amniotic fluid have been seen to help facilitate the repair of spinal discs and bone, and this procedure may be used during spine surgery to aid healing. Amniotic stem cells can also be used to create material for use in fusing or adhering body tissue from one place on the body to another in surgeries. To treat MD, stem cells can be injected into weakened muscle tissue. There, they can supply substances that are missing or in short supply because of gene damage. Although this is still being researched, those with DMD and other NMDs can be encouraged by what the future holds.

Text-Dependent Questions

1. What role does dystrophin play in causing MD?
2. How is the Human Genome Project helpful to researchers studying neuromuscular disorders?
3. What problem can result from attempting to repair an MD gene by injecting muscle tissue from a healthy donor into the weakened MD muscle?

Research Project

Find out and describe how doctors might deal with a patient's rejection of foreign muscle tissue (i.e., tissue from another person).

WORDS TO UNDERSTAND

advocacy: support for or promotion of a cause by a person or group.

assistive technology: equipment to assist a disabled person in carrying out normal activities.

nonprofit organization: an organization that works to help a cause, but not to make money as profit.

CHAPTER FOUR

Meeting the Challenges of NMDs

For most people, being able to move their limbs and joints whenever they want to is an expected part of life. For those who live with an neuromuscular disorder (NMD), however, being unable to move some parts of their bodies can define their lives and sometimes limit their opportunities. Yet people with neuromuscular disorders and similar conditions still achieve amazing things. They meet their challenges in creative ways and join fully into life with those who don't have movement limitations.

Get Educated

The more you know about a problem, the more you can do to meet its challenges. The first major step patients and families can take is to educate themselves about their particular disease. The next is to stay in touch with ongoing developments. Even though relatively few people have neuromuscular diseases, many doctors, researchers, individuals, and organizations across the country are dedicated to finding ways of making life better for all those whose lives are touched by NMD.

Both government and nonprofit organizations provide a wealth of information and opportunities to assist NMD patients and family in finding the facts, services, and other resources they need. Three of them are the Muscular Dystrophy Association (MDA), the Muscular Dystrophy Family Foundation (MDFF), and the National Institutes of Health (NIH). The MDA and MDFF are private, nonprofit organizations, while the NIH is a part of the U.S. Department of Health and Human Services. The NIH is the largest biomedical research agency in the world.

ASSISTIVE TECHNOLOGY

A large number of assistive technology products, such as wheelchairs and scooters, have been developed to offer solutions and physical assistance to people with MD and other neuromuscular disorders. Other available products include canes, stair lifts and standing devices, and aids for eating and drinking, art and writing, sports and gardening, and more.

The USA TechGuide (www. USATechGuide.org) is an online guide to assistive technology products, published by the United Spinal Association (USA). In the TechGuide, you can read other people's reviews of assistive equipment or submit your reviews of products you have used. Reviewing the experiences of others before making a choice among options can be very helpful.

Technology makes it easier for people with movement problems get around more easily.

One of the major ways MDA, MDFF, and NIH help individuals and their families is by providing up-to-date medical information. Medical researchers on university campuses, in government research labs, and in labs of pharmaceutical companies (companies that produce drugs) are constantly searching to discover new information about diseases, as well as looking for new drugs and procedures for coping with or curing diseases.

Nonprofit organizations and **advocacy** groups bring together patients and families, along with medical professionals and researchers. These groups make the public more aware of the diseases and the needs of people with neuromuscular disorders. They also provide support and develop patient-centered information. Many raise funds to support research to find better treatments and pursue cures. The organizations direct interested people to information about research, resources, services, and volunteer opportunities. These groups also have experts who serve as medical advisors. Check pages 40 and 41 to find their websites, where you can learn about the services they offer.

Know Your Rights: The Americans with Disabilities Act

On July 26, 1990, President George H. W. Bush signed the Americans with Disabilities Act (ADA) into law. According to the ADA, a person with a disability is one who has a physical or mental impairment that substantially limits one or more major life activities. The ADA definition of a disabled person also includes a person with a history of such impairment, or the perception by others as being impaired. At the ADA website (ADA.gov), you will find the full text of the ADA, along with resources for assistance in many areas of life for people with disabilities.

The ADA provides grants to many disabled people for specific needs that will help them qualify for jobs. The act makes it illegal for any employer to discriminate against hiring a disabled person for a job they are qualified to do. In fact, the employer is required to modify the workplace in reasonable ways to make it possible for a qualified person who happens to be disabled to work successfully in the job. Disabled persons are able to get help not only with getting a job they're qualified for, but also with getting suitable housing and transportation.

THE AMERICANS WITH DISABILITIES ACT, 1990

"Our success with this act proves that we are keeping faith with the spirit of our courageous forefathers who wrote in the Declaration of Independence: 'We hold these truths to be self-evident, that all men are created equal, that they are endowed by their Creator with certain unalienable rights.' These words have been our guide for more than two centuries as we've labored to form our more perfect union. But tragically, for too many Americans, the blessings of liberty have been limited or even denied. The Civil Rights Act of '64 took a bold step towards righting that wrong. But the stark fact remained that people with disabilities were still victims of segregation and discrimination, and this was intolerable. Today's legislation brings us closer to that day when no Americans will ever again be deprived of their basic guarantee of life, liberty, and the pursuit of happiness.

This act is powerful in its simplicity. It will ensure that people with disabilities are given the basic guarantees for which they have worked so long and so hard: independence, freedom of choice, control of their lives, the opportunity to blend fully and equally into the rich mosaic of the American mainstream. Legally, it will provide our disabled community with a powerful expansion of protections and then basic civil rights. It will guarantee fair and just access to the fruits of American life which we all must be able to enjoy....

Together, we must remove the physical barriers we have created and the social barriers that we have accepted. For ours will never be a truly prosperous nation until all within it prosper."

—Statement of President George H. W. Bush, on the signing of the Americans with Disabilities Act

George H. W. Bush signing the Americans with Disabilities Act in 1990.

Many types of neuromuscular disorders can be disabling to those who must live with them. A visit to ADA.gov can be a valuable step to take for you and your affected family member.

Say YES!

If you have an NMD, don't let your condition stand in the way: say yes to invitations as much as you can. Ask either your home helpers or your hosts for the help you need, such as transportation, in order to accept the opportunity. Saying yes keeps your mind and your world open—and helps you stay part of it.

People with NMD can and should be as self-reliant and independent as possible. But when help is offered, there is nothing wrong with saying yes!

First, many people sincerely want to help. They see that everyone isn't as lucky as they are, and would like to share their good fortune in some way. Second, they sincerely care about the condition and feelings of

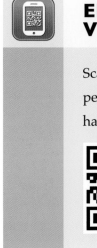

EDUCATIONAL VIDEO

Scan this code for a personal story about having an NMD.

their NMD friend or family member, and they would like to make things easier for that person. And third, for a person with a special disorder, having a core of people who are willing to help and comfortable helping is a valuable asset. These helpers will be there on future occasions when help might genuinely be needed.

Be a Helper

Ironically, people who want to help often need to be helped themselves, in the sense that they need to learn the skills of being an effective helper. There are many skills that can make things go more smoothly. Here are some things to know:

- **Ask first.** If you want to assist someone with an NMD, it's important to ask them how you can help before you jump in. A few examples of ways to ask are:
  - *How can I help?*
  - *May I help you cross the street?*
  - *Shall I hold your arm, or would you prefer to hold mine?*

When talking to someone in a wheelchair, situate yourself at their eye level, rather than looking down at them.

If the person does not want help, stay available, but don't force your help on anyone. The person may have a routine way of performing the task, and unexpected help could actually make things harder rather than easier.

- **Learn how to communicate effectively.** Call things by their correct names. If the person you are helping corrects you, accept the correction and use their preferred terms. Some descriptive words are upsetting or even insulting to people with NMDs. For instance, you may not intend to say anything insulting by using the word "crippled," but your companion may feel insulted. Try to use respectful words like "disabled" rather than "crippled," or simply say, for example, that "John has Becker muscular dystrophy."

- **Speak directly to a person with an NMD.** You'd be surprised how often well-meaning people talk about, around, or over people with an NMD, rather than addressing them directly. If you are talking to someone in a wheelchair, sit at his or her level if possible, rather than leaning awkwardly over them. If a third person is present, include the disabled person in the conversation. Speak to people directly rather than about them to the third person.

- **Don't hesitate to ask questions.** If you are not sure of the best way to interact with someone, just ask!

CONSIDER BEING A VOLUNTEER

Volunteers in research labs make new discoveries possible. Both individuals with healthy muscles and those with NMDs are needed as volunteers to carry out studies of drugs or procedures to cure the disease or lessen its impact. If you have an NMD, consider being a research volunteer to help bring about the cure of your own disorder. However, if you are a family member or friend or just a person who wants to contribute to ending a cruel disease, a wide range of volunteer opportunities are available to assist in research or in patient organizations. You can find information about volunteering at the MDA, MDFF, and NIH websites.

Take Charge! An Empowering Way of Thinking

When someone is diagnosed with an NMD, it can be tempting to feel self-pity and a sense of hopelessness. However, not everyone thinks that way. Those who choose to take charge of their own lives are choosing to build a positive, upbeat life in spite of their circumstances. Medical research has not yet given them the power to control their muscular disorder, but they *can* control how they respond to their situation. They've decided to take up

Team sports are a great way for people with NMDs to stay as active as possible.

A medical condition is not an identity: someone with an NMD is still a son, a brother, and an important member of the family.

the challenge of finding new ways to do the things their muscles won't do for them yet. They have the power to enjoy the people and organizations dedicated to assisting them in living fully every day. They can study each day and follow developments in the search for treatments and, eventually, cures for their disorders. They can say yes to the invitations and opportunities that come their way. They can encourage others to become more compassionate, thoughtful people by gently, and compassionately, teaching them positive, effective ways of helping.

A number of organizations designed to make life more positive for people with special difficulties have named themselves Take Charge! Two are related to particular medical conditions: multiple sclerosis (www.mscando.org/multiple-sclerosis-programs/take-charge) and hydrocephalus (www.hydroassoc.org/tag/teens-take-charge). Like MD, these conditions are, at this time, incurable. Both organizations offer support, companionship, and positive life approaches to living every day to the fullest. DMD and NMD patients can also take charge in their own lives and choose to make difficulties into challenges that strengthen them every day.

Text-Dependent Questions

1. Name three different online organizations or agencies where you can get answers to your questions about MD.
2. What services does the MDA offer?
3. What are three types of assistive equipment that could be helpful to some MD patients?

Research Project

What steps could you take to safely find and correspond online with a person who has the same diagnosis as you? Find this new friend. Through your exchange of experiences, find out something you didn't know about your disorder.

FURTHER READING

Burcaw, Shane. *Laughing at My Nightmare*. New York: Roaring Brook Press, 2014.

Emery, Alan E. H., *Muscular Dystrophy*. 4th ed. New York: Oxford University Press, 2015.

Fabian, Cynthia. *Erica's Tripod: A Book about a Girl with Muscular Dystrophy*. Durham, CT: Strategic Book Publishing, 2014.

Hoffman Van Benthuysen, Cory. "The Hidden Hurts of Sibling Support." *Quest*. January 1, 2004. http://quest.mda.org/article/hidden-hurts-sibling-support.

Mayo Clinic Staff. "Muscular Dystrophy." http://www.mayoclinic.org/diseases-conditions/muscular-dystrophy/basics/definition/con-20021240.

Sutton, Amy L., ed. *Disabilities Sourcebook*. 2nd ed. Detroit, MI: Omnigraphics, 2011.

Tudin, Shelley. *You're Too Cute to be Disabled: Living with Limb-Girdle Muscular Dystrophy*. iUniverse, 2012.

Van Benthuysen, Mandy. "Living with Limb-Girdle Muscular Dystrophy." https://www.mda.org/disease/limb-girdle-muscular-dystrophy/living-with.

Educational Videos

Chapter One: John Graybill II. "Limb-Girdle Muscular Dystrophy 2A: Walking." https://youtu.be/TKL5krEsiVI.

Chapter Two: Sciencentral. "Muscular Dystrophy Drug." https://youtu.be/MQHGKZZ6wno.

Chapter Three: Parent Project Muscular Dystrophy. "End Duchenne: Time Is Ticking." https://youtu.be/qETzEeUA6xE.

Chapter Four: Pfunk Jr. "My Muscular Dystrophy Story." https://youtu.be/68YO2eh1bIY.

SERIES GLOSSARY

accommodation: an arrangement or adjustment to a new situation; for example, schools make accommodations to help students cope with illness.

anemia: an illness caused by a lack of red blood cells.

autoimmune: type of disorder where the body's immune system attacks the body's tissues instead of germs.

benign: not harmful.

biofeedback: a technique used to teach someone how to control some bodily functions.

capillaries: tiny blood vessels that carry blood from larger blood vessels to body tissues.

carcinogens: substances that can cause cancer to develop.

cerebellum: the back part of the brain; it controls movement.

cerebrum: the front part of the brain; it controls many higher-level thinking and functions.

cholesterol: a waxy substance associated with fats that coats the inside of blood vessels, causing cardiovascular disease.

cognitive: related to conscious mental activities, such as learning and thinking.

communicable: transferable from one person to another.

congenital: a condition or disorder that exists from birth.

correlation: a connection between different things that suggests they may have something to do with one another.

dominant: in genetics, a dominant trait is expressed in a child even when the trait is only inherited from one parent.

environmental factors: anything that affects how people live, develop, or grow. Climate, diet, and pollution are examples.

genes: units of hereditary information.

hemorrhage: bleeding from a broken blood vessel.

hormones: substances the body produces to instruct cells and tissues to perform certain actions.

inflammation: redness, swelling, and tenderness in a part of the body in response to infection or injury.

insulin: a hormone produced in the pancreas that controls cells' ability to absorb glucose.

lymphatic system: part of the human immune system; transports white blood cells around the body.

malignant: harmful; relating to tumors, likely to spread.

mutation: a change in the structure of a gene; some mutations are harmless, but others may cause disease.

neurological: relating to the nervous system (including the brain and spinal cord).

neurons: specialized cells found in the central nervous system (the brain and spinal cord).

occupational therapy: a type of therapy that teaches one how to accomplish tasks and activities in daily life.

oncology: the study of cancer.

orthopedic: dealing with deformities in bones or muscles.

prevalence: how common or uncommon a disease is in any given population.

prognosis: the forecast for the course of a disease that predicts whether a person with the disease will get sicker, recover, or stay the same.

progressive disease: a disease that generally gets worse as time goes on.

psychomotor: relating to movement or muscle activity resulting from mental activity.

recessive: in genetics, a recessive trait will only be expressed if a child inherits it from both parents.

remission: an improvement in or disappearance of someone's symptoms of disease; unlike a cure, remission is usually temporary.

resilience: the ability to bounce back from difficult situations.

seizure: an event caused by unusual brain activity resulting in physical or behavior changes.

syndrome: a condition with a set of associated symptoms.

ulcers: a break or sore in skin or tissue where cells disintegrate and die. Infections may occur at the site of an ulcer.

INDEX

Illlustrations are indicated by page numbers in *italic* type.

ABOUT THE ADVISOR

Heather Pelletier, Ph.D., is a pediatric staff psychologist at Rhode Island Hospital/Hasbro Children's Hospital with a joint appointment as a clinical assistant professor in the departments of Psychiatry and Human Behavior and Pediatrics at the Warren Alpert Medical School of Brown University. She is also the director of behavioral pain medicine in the division of Children's Integrative therapies, Pain management and Supportive care (CHIPS) in the department of Pediatrics at Hasbro Children's Hospital. Dr. Pelletier provides clinical services to children in various medical specialty clinics at Hasbro Children's Hospital, including the pediatric gastroenterology, nutrition, and liver disease clinics.

ABOUT THE AUTHOR

Molly Jones was a high school teacher for six years and is now a freelance writer of nonfiction for young people. She has written a number of books for the publishers Rosen and Child's World, and often writes about health care topics.

PHOTO CREDITS